My story of Strongholds.

Chazaray S. Henderson

Introduction

My Burdens and Strongholds is a book written in the midst of many trials, situations, emotions and encounters in my life. I wrote this book to extend a hand to many different people that are going through some difficult things in life that others may not quite understand. I know what it's like to be misunderstood, confused, stressed, addicted, frustrated, locked up, and in bondage. The Iniquities within Life, was completed in the midst of me finding myself. It took 28 years of my life for me to realize who I really was. I've suffered many times in life because of my own foolish decision making. I'm not proud of my past, although I wouldn't take any of it back because It's develop me into who I am today mentally. The first step is to want to change. Change takes place when you are tired of crying, hurting, and being burdened of all the wicked manifestations within the heart. God is the answer, but you have to remember that nothing happens overnight, everything is a process. Never strive to make change to satisfy people. It's not sincere and you will always end up battling in your mind, ending up back where you started, or worst. Make changes for yourself and not for others to see. As bad as we desire for people that are close to us to understand, or feel what we're going through. They can't always comprehend, so this causes us to become very frustrated at times. Our life stories are for us to remember, in order to keep us from going back to those depressing, stressful, long suffering days and nights of our past. I'll tell you a secret that helped me a lot. You know how in most cases we are taught to blame the devil, or rebuke the devil? I realize that my life was so off track because of my own mindset. We make choices on our own, and we suffer for them, no matter what these choices may be. Wherever you are in your life right now, you must understand that you put yourself in that position, or maybe you allowed someone else to influence or manipulate you into that particular situation. Either way, everyone has to actually think about a decision before an action takes place. Acknowledge your downfalls and strongholds and remove from those sources. You have suffered long enough, so don't wait until it's too late. I tried to define myself in everyone I looked up to because I didn't have a father. Maybe you have neither mother nor father. Just remember, resolving an issue, is getting down to the root of it first. Get somewhere quiet and alone to retrace your life back to where it started, which is "The Root". Always seek God for yourself, and if you don't know him, make sure that you allow the right person to teach you. This is very important because many of us have been misled and lied to by our leaders, which cause many to turn away from the very source, and last source we may have at times. This causes us to become rebellious and confused, pursuing businesses, positions, and purposes that God never had in store for our lives. This creates more burdens, separation, frustrations and confusion within our minds, homes, marriages, churches, relationships, committees, and ministries. Again, I will tell you, don't wait until it is too late. The next time you may end up somewhere that you don't want to be or a grave you can't turn back from.

Proverbs 29:1

He that being often reproved hardeneth his neck, shall suddenly be destroyed, and without remedy.

Table of contents

Trying to escape myself

All these dark days and deeply engraved issues living within these bars, with mental scars,

Of all of the pain I've caused,

To my family, and all of the people I love, that love me back dearly,

My heart cries out, "I'm sorry, sincerely."

I feel like a monster sometimes and if you don't want to get hurt, then don't come near me,

I'm so tired of being ignorant, my heart has grown so weary,

I'm so sick of crying,

My days have been shorten, so I know I'm dying,

I just want to become consistent about doing things right,

So tired of hiding from God in the day, and lurking in the night,

I want to shed so many tears, because of the loss of many years,

Going to hell and burning forever are my only fears,

All the times I got high to make myself feel better, and to forget about the beast I had become,

Just like Adam and Eve, I run and run and run,

But I could still hear God's voice, finally realizing that I can't hide from God,

So I had no choice, but to abide, in his ways,

I've struggled so long trying to escape the evil desires that my flesh craved,

I admit the devil has had a grip on me, way to long,

I was content of the fact that hell would be my home,

Some kind of way, I have to get free,

Free from all these familiar demons that strive to destroy me,

They've ruined my life and sabotaged my reputation,

Evil schemes have always been constant contemplations,

God it feels like I'm already in some kind of hell,

Just sitting here at this very moment, in a cell, trying to tell,
My life story,

God please help me change, so that I can give the glory.

Transitions

I will always give reverence to the most high,

It's been an extremely long process discovering my purpose before I die,
Lurking in those streets that once was my main focus and my home,

Although my conscious always convicted me and would never leave me alone,
Growing up was so frustrating, I was so confused about life,

My heart was flooded with so much anger and strife,

My hands dealt so many mistakes causing me to suffer from my own decisions, going back and forth to jail,

A fiend to my rebellious ways that destined my soul for Hell,

Only a living God could see me through all these mental phases,

For so long I was ashamed of God, withholding so many of his praises,

Arrogant and so stubborn, playing around in those deadly streets,

Lying and deceiving women, just to lie between their sheets,

Not realizing there was a table already prepared for me,

My addictions and habits made me lame in the eyes, so I was too blind to see,

I'd strived so hard to develop a reputation amongst these heathens,

The same reputation that has made my life so difficult, for so many different reasons,
I used to be convinced, that the dark paths of this world was the lifestyle for me,
If only I would have known, how hard it would be to get free,

Free from these demons that attached themselves to my mindset,

The strongholds, addictions, and ties of the lust and sex,

Fortunately I've been allowed the opportunity to look back over my deceitful past,

How could God be so forgiving, sparing my life when I constantly put him last?

For so long in my suffering, he never left me alone,

Now I have children that define themselves within the walls of my life,

It's amazing how some things can convince us to change and do what's right;
So foolish all them years, just to become a nobody,

Now when I have nothing, in my children's eyes I'm somebody,

I'm so glad that I have found my way back to the paths my mother taught me that I should go,
In life we will always reap the things we soe.

Changes

There always comes the days we have to face the consequences of the seeds we've sown,

Reaping will surely sprout on the grounds you planted them on,

Our deception, burdens and heart aches we've brought amongst others,

Along with our sick ways of thinking that disgrace our fathers and shame our mothers,

So many exotic seeds implanted within us by our peers,

Creating issues that have corrupted us for so many years,

The pain of hardship and suffering repeatedly, from our own stupid mistakes,

Constantly being punished for all the wickedness we demonstrate,

Bald up in the agony of our decisions, forced to make changes within ourselves,

Seeking to fulfill voids can be like drawing water from dry wells,

Many of us experienced so much pain in life, words really can't describe,

Misled, betrayed, confused, and abandoned by so many of our role models that portrayed us lies,

There will always come a day in life when we just get sick of these pains,

And when we get tired enough, then comes "Change".

The Bondage of Friends

We use to be inseparable and no one could tear us apart,

I accepted you in my life and made room for you in my heart,

In my eyes, you could never do me wrong or do anything to betray me,

I loved you just like a siblings, and we interacted daily,

Introduced to a fast life at extremely young ages,

Fatherless with no one to define ourselves in, so we went through many phases,

We wore each other clothes, and our parents were close friends,

All the fun we had, we used to wish it would never end,

We pursued a lifestyle of drugs, and followed in the path of our downfalls,

Thinking we could win, prevailing in the darkness, going hard and never paused,

I've brought dark clouds of shame upon my mother's house, causing her many nights of tears,

For so many years,

Families and friends we've shattered and torn, behind these drugs just to stimulate a feeling,

We became so ruthless and remorseless, and numb to who we were killing,

We lost so many friends since we've grown up, that are now deceased,

I sabotaged my life for so long, because of the friends I couldn't seem to release.

Never Thought

I've experienced so many frustrating and stressful moments in life, that only seemed to get worse,

Although it's my own fault, constantly submitting to my downfalls first,

My own self destruction,

It seems as if stress and frustration, came together and conceived more issues through reproduction,

Could life really get any more painful?

Having to face my own calamity, causing me to feel so shameful,

Defining myself in the mindset and mentalities of my peers,

Struggling not knowing who I really was, for so many valuable years,

So many trips to jail and uncontrollable tears,

I still dwell on the many people that had hope in me that I disappointed,

For so long I despised sniffing cocaine, but I never thought that I'd ever be high on it,

Chasing the drains and never stopped to think about where the lines would cause me to end up,
I Never knew how hard it would be to depose of a mindset that was once so corrupt,

Never thought I would be so good at committing so many crimes,

Never thought I would help destroy the lives of so many that are already dying,

I Never thought that I'd see myself crying.

Feeling my way through the darkness

Throughout my whole life I've made so many stupid choices,

The choices to heed all the wrong voices,

Cursing my decease father out while he lay in his grave because of so much grief and anger,

From being confused and no one to define myself in but danger,

The dangers of being consumed by my adversaries dwelling amongst me that were destroying my mind,
Ruining my purpose and misleading me as though I was blind,

I Couldn't seem to find the path, my mother once taught me that I should go as a child,

So young and frustrated, carrying the weight of my heavy burdens repeatedly up the church isles,
To the altar so many times begging for forgiveness, weeping and crying,
So many moments I just wanted to end everything and just stop trying,

Although I was to scared to fulfill the suicidal thoughts that manifested in my head,

The fears of just handing my soul over to the demons I've constantly fled,

I've spent my whole life trying to escape from the bondage and consequences I created by myself,
Only God can come save me, because I have no one else.

Powder Cocaine

One of the most painful feelings I've had was letting go of this close friend I once loved so dearly,

The withdrawals caused me to feel so sad and weary,

Why was it so hard to let go of the things that were slowly killing me?

Some way, I had to break free,

From the strongholds and addictions stealing me,

Away from my family,

We've gotten so high together and done so many adventurous things,

Not realizing how much hurt, separation, and troubles cocaine would bring,

Often times I made quick decisions, not acknowledging who all they would affect, or what could go wrong,
Cocaine caused me to forget the priorities and responsibilities within my home,

Nothing really mattered, when we where together,

Coming down from you was so depressing, so I tried to chase your high forever,

I've hurt so many people that loved me, and burned so many bridges for you,

You were like a nightmare that came true,

It took years before I actually realized, how abusive and thoughtless you've caused me to be,

I can't believe how much cocaine changed me,

So high and carefree, cocaine draining like a river inside of my head, poisoning my mind,

I had to leave you alone, because you had me blind,

Blind to my kids, and remorseless in the pain I've caused others,

Even stealing from my own mother,

I might have even disappointed you,

I used to be in denial, but now I can admit, that I was addicted and never knew.

A Man of Many Faces

I've had some good days, and even more bad,

At times I've been so happy and many times I've been sad,

I've seen days my smile was bright as the sun,

I've also been overwhelmed with pain and tears, because of the bad things I've done,

I been in the presence of my mighty living God,

I've also been punished and corrected, many times by his rod,

I've done so many things in my life, because I was free,

I've been locked up behind concrete and steel bars, that limited my eyes to the things I could see,

I've been high on powder cocaine,

I've been drowned in my tears of shame,

I've experienced striving to do right and going to church,

Although it brought so many disappointments and hurts,

I've been in the midst of ministers and preachers,

I've been suicidal and so close to death, in the presence of my reaper,

I've done so many things that seem right in my eyes,

Once upon a time, I've told so many lies,

I've been homeless and lacked much needed resources,

I've been possessed by so many demonic forces,

I've prevailed with my enemies, and people that have continuously betrayed me,

I once had so much potential, that seems to drain away daily,

I've tried to define myself, in so many different faces,

I've been misled so many times, and ended up in all the wrong places,

I've been strong and healthy as could be,

I've been full of filth and STD,

I've been mentally blind and lame.

I’ve been hopeless and alone with no one else to blame,

I’ve caused so much heartache and heavy burdens,

I’ve chose to seclude myself from the light, hiding behind closed curtains,

I’ve fought with my own issues and strived to break loose from addictions I’ve once denied,

Staggering from a high, that I just can’t hide,

Struggling to overcome the mindset of myself,

I’ve burned so many bridges till I could neither turn to the right or left.

Roots of my Ancestors

Entangled in my roots, and tormented by my ancestors demons,

Strangled by pain, distress, and this anger that has took a toll on my life for so many different reasons,
Prevailing in the pitch dark paths of my peers,

As a young boy, I defined myself in my adversaries, for so many painful years,

Immune and so familiar walking in the dark paths at such a young age,

Couldn't define myself in a deceased father, so I developed demonic ways,

From the demons that were cursed, upon the ground I walk,

A mind corrupted and overflowing with so many evil thoughts,

Why did I keep giving in, to the very things that were designed to destroy me?

My enemy is like a loud voice in my head, that constantly annoys me,

Striving to escape from myself, before I run out time,

For years tradition has taught me to blame the devil, and those doctrines kept me blind,

Blind from whom my enemy really was, and where my issues sprouted,

For years I gave up on God and doubted,

I traced everything I've struggled with, back to my roots,

Sometimes that's the only way we can find the answers to breaking loose

Tears

Tears are like rain, except they are developed from deep within,
Deep in the heart, where God balances our sins,
Many of our tears have formed from of dark clouds of pain,
Hard suffering and shame, who else can I blame?
For my own thoughtless decisions and mistakes, quick to demonstrate,
Evil works but not thinking about what lies await,
Dark clouds hang over my head,
Suicidal thoughts and wishing I was dead,
Chastised and disciplined, by our heavenly Father,
Sometimes we learn things the hard way, because we make life harder,
Not thinking about the others that love us at all,
So many people I've disappointed, and all the grief I've caused,
How can I bring tears upon my eyes, and tears to yours too?
So many people you've let down, that once trusted you.
I'm Sorry....

Putting God Last

I've always had knowledge of my living God, I was just too busy fulfilling my own desires,

I can't say that I've always loved God, if I did I would be a liar,
when the world is revolving around me, he never crossed my mind,

But yet and still when I'm bound, he seems to always be the only light I find,

Why do I submit to these wicked ways? I wonder what it's going to take?

My mindset has such a grip on me, I just can't shake.

When you have no one Else

The weight of life bares down hard on my mind mentally,

Being so frustrated and misunderstood, has caused me to deceive the laws of man, intentionally,

A corrupt mind frame, that has been created and developed, by all of my peers,

I've struggled so long to readjust my violent and foolish ways of thinking, for many years,

I'm striving to make a change, but no one believes me,

Where I am in life, God is the only source who can tame me,

I have no one else to call on, and no one else to turn to,

I have burned all my bridges, so now Lord I guess it is just me an you.....

Searching

Lord, I've been in many dark places searching for you, high and low,

I've searched for you in friends, but they betrayed and abandoned me, leaving me nowhere to go,
I've cried out to you time after time, alone in secret places,

So many have come in your name, although they were all the wrong faces,
I've been to so many different types of church,
I just knew I would find you there, but instead I found hurt,
I've fallen many times in a process striving to walk,
Trying to keep my head up, has been a battle that I've constantly fought,
I really need for you to show up, I have no one else to turn to,
Lord, I don't trust anyone now; so this time it's going to have to be you.

The best at failing

I never was any good at anything, other than making dumb mistakes,
I despised morals, and followed in the paths of foolish men that boasted and prate,

I never succeeded at many things, I would take the easy way out or quit,
So puzzled growing up, striving to force my way in places I would never fit,
Bound with thick steel chains and wicked desires of my own flesh,

When it came to burning bridges and relationships, I was the best,

I always wanted to turn away from sin, although I was bond from the heart,
How could I have avoided my deceitful ways, when I lacked so much from the start,
I felt so worthless, I was determined that there was no hope for me,
But only God could purge me, molding me into the man he designed me to be.

Manifestation of a Stronghold

Life is full of strongholds and downfalls that grab hold to us from birth,

Creating a mindset that develops addictions, bringing afflictions that only get worse,

Then comes the grip of bondage latching on to us without permission,

Ignorance fulfills the emptiness of our voids causing us to make repeated mistakes and thoughtless decisions,

The decisions that have permanently engraved our names in the system,

The days of our lives are very valuable although many of us took chances and risk them,

One more felony away from prison or one more gauge away from an overdose,

Or what about the cocaine addiction that links you in your friends close,

One more partner away from Aids,

Always boasting and bragging about how many times you've got laid,

Vulnerability breaks us down and reduces the level of our standards,

Leaving us with no one to blame for our own reputations we've sabotaged and slandered.

Addictions

I want to change so bad, I'm so sick of these streets,

I consume more drugs than the food I eat,

What have I done to myself? I look twice my age,

I invest into my downfalls and addictions every time I receive a wage,

I just can't seem to function without drugs; my body is so immune,

I use to have a house and family but now I live from hotel room to motel room,

I use to have morals but now I think I've lost my mind,

Life never goes my way so I just stop trying,

I choose to get high thinking I'll forget my problems,

Although I would have to stay high forever, in order to solve them,

I used to use drugs for fun now I think I need it,

It's almost like oxygen and I can't live if I can't breathe it,

How could I allow an addiction to consume everything I've had?

I never realized how small I've gotten, man I look bad.

I've been there

No one knows where I've been in life, no one understands,

"I'm like this close" to killing myself and I'm not playing,

I'm so sick of crying,

I give up; I'm tired of trying,

To do things right, in spite, of all the negative influences around me,

All their sarcasm and criticism, that seems to drown me,

I've sown a whole field of bad seeds,

So everything I reap causes me to grieve,

I've burnt so many close relationships and bridges down,

It just seems like life isn't worth living now,

I always make the stupidest mistakes,

Sometimes I hate,

Myself, and I wish that God never put me here,

I hope my dying day is getting near,

I can't seem to find any real friends,

They constantly come and go, betraying me again and again,

I can't seem to find real help in the church,

They just burden me with more sadness, disappointments and hurts,

I'd rather sniff some cocaine and chase my high,

No one can keep it real they just procrastinate and lie,

Maybe I'll go smoke some weed,

Maybe that can relieve,

My stress,

Or maybe I'll pick up this 9mm, and lay my own self down to rest.

I'm Sorry Ma

Mama I'm sorry that I didn't ever listen,

All you were trying to do was keep me out of prison,

I was so rebellious, walking in the paths of my friends,

I caused you so much pain; you probably thought the aches would never come to an end,

I remember like it was yesterday, you was laying my cloths out for school,

I started selling dope out your house leaving you disappointed and confused,

I'm so sorry I caused you so many stressful nights and tears to your eyes,

And all of my stealing and telling lies,

You just wanted me to grow up; you wanted me to be a man,

Just grow up and be wise with a plan,

I can still hear you crying because it hurted you to put me out,

All the fussing and yelling, I can still hear your screams and shouts,

I put so many burdens on you; the thought of this makes me cry,

I tried to kill myself in your house because I just wanted to die,

You introduced me to the Lord and raised me up in the church,

You taught me the way I should go and brought you back hurts,

I was like Satan in your house,

I remember being angry with my father for dying and cursing him with my mouth,

I caused you to loose so much hope in me,

I know at times you probably thought that you would have to bury me,

You've bailed me out of jail, so many times,

You never thought I would be on cocaine, sniffing lines,

I've brought so many guns in your house and I even stole from you,

You stood in way of God, because of what you didn't want me to go through,

Just like a mama always running to her child's rescue,

And the more you did the more I disappointed you,

I'm sorry mama, for so many years of shame,

God has brought you through so much; I'm surprised that you are still sane,

All the embarrassing times my face had showed up on the news,

Running the streets trying to impress these fools,

I can remember you coming home from work and I'm sitting in the back of police cars,

I'm sorry I engraved you with so many mental scars,

I'm so sorry; it took so long to get myself right,

Now everyday I strive to be a real man with all my might.

The Trail

Growing up as a young man I stumbled across many roles,

Molding and shaping my failures and developing my potential goals,

I searched for an identity in the people that I thought were my friends,

My voids opened my heart up to the wicked ways of men,

I've made so many instant decisions,

Causing me some painful afflictions,

I use to be a follower walking in unfamiliar trails,

Taking my family through so many different stages of hell,

This world is a 100% pure and more poignant than a drug,

The consequences of our choices will show us no love,

We will always reap every bad seed we've sown,

Where will our paths take us? We never have known,

These paths could lead us to prison or maybe to our graves,

The environments we identify ourselves in affect us in many ways,

Some of us had to learn the hard way; some died and was made an example,

Many became addicted to a stronghold trying their first sample.

My Shame

My shame,

Developed from many years of pain,

The people that put me on a petal stool, I took them through so many changes,

Sitting in jail so many times full of anger and blameless,

Living on the streets, selling dope,

Remorseless, with no hope, didn't care if I was killing folk,

Breaking in houses and always stealing,

Trying to stay high so that I would be numb to my feelings,

Sleeping in my car with nowhere to live,

Sleeping in breezeways because my friends couldn't keep it real,

Taking my family for granted and making them cry,

9mm to my head just wishing I could die,

Then back to jail again,

Needed bail money but I couldn't find my friends,

I've been stabbed in the back so many times,

So full of rebellious ways and a expert committing crimes,

I've lain at many altars, praying that God would change me,

Locked up again because no one could tame me,

Sniffing all those grams of cocaine,

Can't even feel my nose but still trying to catch a drain,

Tired of suffering in bondage of these invisible demons,

I turned my back on my heavenly father, for no reason,

My peers tried to warn me but I never would listen,

It was always something out there, I thought I was missing.

From top to bottom

I used to think selling dope was the best way of living,

I didn't care about getting caught and going to prison,

I went through this phase trying to be just like my peers,

Even though they were already locked up, serving many years,

I used to love the fast life and all the money and the cars,

I never thought about how hard it would be adapting to life behind bars,

All the fake friends that seemed to appear from mid air,

When I really needed them not a single one was there,

It's amazing how everybody wants to chill when they think you got a little change,

But when you're broke and struggling, none of them can help you with a single thing.

The Pain of Decisions

My Life was paved by my decisions, where did yours take you?

Our decisions are the reasons; we go through the things we go through,

We all have choices to who determines our future,

Some straddle God's path and many submit to the ways of Lucifer,

Our decisions have put in so many dispositions,

So many people tried to warn us, but we wouldn't listen,

These decisions have sabotaged our reputations and we've slandered our names,

People judge you according to your past; they said you'd never change,

It was your choice of your addictions,

So you chose your outcome and afflictions,

You made the choice to impress your friends,

Not realizing how much trouble you'd get in,

We put ourselves within the walls of a jail,

We make the decisions to succeed or fail,

You bound yourself in those chains,

You thought life was all about fun and games,

You made these decisions so why do you blame,

Everyone else for your pain?

Trying to Change

Lord help me to stay focused; don't let me get off track,

So many demons are after me, they want my soul back,

I didn't think I would ever escape,

They want me to burn with them, they can't wait,

I tried to sell my soul to Satan at a young age,

I've destroyed and sabotaged my life in so many ways,

Lord please keep your hands on me,

I just want to be a man although this process gets very lonely,

I've been in so many dark places, alone and depressed,

I can hear demons talking to me; I think they're in my flesh,

How can I overcome them, they still have this hold on me,

Lord did you destine me for hell because I just can't seem to get free.

Weary

I've made so many terrible mistakes,

So why should I believe something is within me that's so great,

I've caused tremendous heartaches and stress,

If I didn't do evil, I couldn't rest,

I've let so many people within my family down,

They were grieved and burdened, whenever I came around,

I was very unstable within my mind,

I was so stupid, so I never had my chance to really shine,

My head covered with my sheets, just weeping and crying,

Everyday is just a closer day, to me dying.

The Season of fall

It seems like I've been falling since the age of eleven,

Like Satan and his demons fell out of heaven,

I've fell so many times to the waist side,

I still have so many issues because my flesh hasn't died,

I submitted myself to so many evil things as a little man,

God tried to rescue me several times, but I ran and ran,

I have disobeyed God's laws and have not abided,

I've struggled with some evil ways and I can not hide it,

I've been bound within these filthy walls,

When will this season end, of this great fall?

Running

I was swift to run and hide in a dark place,

When God would seek after me, I would hide my face,

I ran and hid in my high,

I've hid by telling a lie,

I ran from my feelings, I hardened my heart,

I tried to do things purposely to keep me and God apart,

I ran to so many of my downfalls and adversaries,

I never thought I would lie in a casket in a mortuary.

Dedication

This Book is Dedicated to everyone that has encountered hardships, depression, frustration, bondage and being misunderstood. I would like to thank God, as well as the very few people that supported me in this journey I've been though to get here. Never take life for granted and always learn from your mistakes, DON'T REPEAT THEM...

CHAZARAY S. HENDERSON

Proverbs 29:1

He that being often reproved hardeneth his neck, shall suddenly be destroyed, and without remedy

www.ingramcontent.com/pod-product-compliance
Ingram Content Group UK Ltd.
Pitfield, Milton Keynes, MK11 3LW, UK
UKHW051133260726
13967UKWH00010B/3019

9 781105 479472